Targeted Killing

Since October 2018, United States international security policy has been held hostage and deprived of intellectual nourishment. An orchestrated propaganda campaign took hold of the nation's capital in response to the assassination in Istanbul of Jamal Khashoggi, a member of Saudi Arabia's wealthy and politically powerful oligarchy.

In death, Khashoggi became known to millions of consumers of Western mainstream media who had never before heard of the man nor thought on an informed basis about the complex issues of Middle Eastern politics and security. He was described as a courageous journalist. He was mourned as a martyred advocate of radical reform in Saudi Arabia. He was hailed as a champion of democracy and human rights as they are proclaimed in the West.

Day after day and week after week, the same reports of his gruesome killing led the coverage of CNN, the *Washington Post*, and other influential outlets. It was as though Bill Murray's clock radio on Groundhog Day had been programmed to broadcast *Saturday Night Live*'s old running gag about Generalissimo Franco still being deceased – except it wasn't funny. A human being had been murdered, and the foul deed was metastasizing into an "international incident" challenging the very underpinnings of some of the world's most vital security relationships.

At the beginning of the wall-to-wall coverage, before it was even confirmed that Khashoggi had been killed and not merely abducted alive, a coordinated message burst forth from the voices of the media and many American politicians, both Republicans and Democrats. Before it was clear exactly what crime had been committed, the villains in the case were named. Two major world political figures were placed in the dock of public opinion, prosecuted in a multimedia show trial, and recommended for career-ending penalties: Saudi Arabia's de facto ruler Crown

---

Khashoggi's assassination, if one is to be realistic about it, fits into the international political category of "targeted killing."

Prince Mohammed bin Salman and U.S. president Donald Trump.

A formerly unknown Saudi oligarch was suddenly elevated to the altars of secular liberalism as a sort of Albert Schweitzer, Mother Teresa, and Nelson Mandela rolled into one. The Saudi prince was proclaimed the savage who ordered the killing, and Trump was told to make a major break in U.S.-Saudi relations or else be indicted by "world opinion" as an accomplice in the crime of the century.

In December, U.S. senators, in one of the feel-good gestures of bipartisan non-legislation for which they have become so famously unpopular, took their stand in an anonymous "voice vote" on a resolution condemning the Saudi crown prince as the prime global evildoer of the moment. Individual senators have called explicitly for his removal from office – in other words, regime change.

Only a few months earlier, Crown Prince Mohammed's dramatic reform campaign had been the toast of the West's fickle liberal intellectualoids. Some realistic conservatives had taken cautious encouragement from the prince's efforts too, and rightly so. Prince Mohammed had declared his determination to align Saudi Arabia with "moderate Islam" and to combat radical political Islamists ranging from the Muslim Brotherhood to Al Qaeda and ISIS. He introduced some social reforms and accelerated efforts to diversify the national economy from heavy dependence on oil. He also made unprecedented gestures towards introducing greater tolerance and freedom for the millions of Christian guest workers in his country, and he showed signs of amity towards the State of Israel too.

For Western liberals, the death of Jamal Khashoggi transformed their view of Prince

Mohammed. Overnight the prince went from reformer to reprobate, from a symbol of hope to a caricature of the Middle Eastern despotic monster.

What is going on here?

Khashoggi's assassination, if one is to be realistic about it, fits into the international political category of "targeted killing." This sort of extrajudicial killing, often on foreign soil, of persons considered to threaten vital national security interests is conducted routinely these days by the United States and Israel. These assassinations, to understate the matter, are controversial within the circles of international law. Yet those with the will and the power to perform them go on doing so.

Every such assassination, whether executed by a drone or a human hit team, is gruesome. Every such killing leaves holes in the hearts of innocent children, spouses, lovers, and friends of the deceased. Still, that does not mean that Israel and the United States are inherently immoral when they commit such killings.

There is no simple moral equivalence

between one targeted killing and another. Reasonable people employing sound moral reasoning might find certain assassinations carried out by the Israelis and Americans justifiable while finding Khashoggi's assassination unjustifiable. But from the Saudi leaders' perspective, the action was a targeted killing of an individual they considered a threat to their kingdom's national security.

What is clearly morally wrong and dangerous to millions of innocent people here and in the Middle East is the emotionally charged campaign to pressure the U.S. government to support the overthrow of the ruler of Saudi Arabia. No good can come of such recklessness.

The euphoria concerning the young, reforming Saudi crown prince just a few months ago was not a sober stance. Worse still is the "Off with his head!" attitude towards the prince of naïve U.S. politicians of both parties.

Mood swings in international relations are dangerous – extremely dangerous when they take place at the heart of the government of the world's leading superpower.

Sometimes it appears that what is taking place is a targeted killing of judiciously decided U.S. national security policy. Or maybe it's better to call it an assisted suicide, with the Kevorkian role performed by sentimental humanitarians named Corker, Flake, Graham, and Rubio.

My Lunch with Jamal Khashoggi

Jamal Khashoggi was a very charming person. I learned this directly in March 2012 when I attended an international public relations conference in Dubai. I took the last open seat at one of the luncheon tables, and it happened that the man seated at my right was Jamal Khashoggi.

I had lived and worked in Saudi Arabia since 2009, and I knew the outline of Khashoggi's career. He was the scion of one of the wealthiest families in Saudi Arabia and a tremendously privileged member of the Saudi power structure. An uncle, the arms dealer Adnan Khashoggi, had been a billionaire global playboy celebrity whose heyday was the 1980s, when a billion dollars was a lot of money. Jamal Khashoggi had a pleasant voice and a merry twinkle in his eye – and wouldn't you, too, if the world were your oyster?

He enjoyed his life and his work. In Saudi Arabia he had a high public profile, unusual

---

Mood swings in international relations are extremely dangerous when they take place at the heart of the government of the world's leading superpower.

---

for one who was not a member of the royal family. He had been a writer and editor for Saudi newspapers and a news presenter on

Saudi TV. Among those who follow international politics, it was no secret that he was also one of the closest advisers to the senior prince who was longtime head of the Saudi state intelligence and secret police apparatus. At times he was overtly on the staff of the Saudi intelligence agency and of Saudi embassies.

All media enterprises in Saudi Arabia are owned or controlled by the government and members of the Saudi royal family. At least until he went to live in the United States in late 2017, all of Khashoggi's writings and utterances, no matter how nuanced they may have been calculated to appear or sound, were completely controlled by strict Saudi government dictate and censorship.

Khashoggi and I had a lengthy conversation, and he spoke expansively of a new assignment he was undertaking. He had been hired to establish and manage Al-Arab, a new, Saudi-controlled television news network that was intended to compete with Qatar's enormously successful Al Jazeera. It was to be headquartered in the island country of Bahrain, just across the King Fahd Causeway from the Eastern Province of Saudi Arabia.

Locating in Bahrain would allow "greater ease of doing business," Khashoggi told me, explaining that expat personnel and interview subjects would be much more comfortable living in, or traveling in and out of, the more carefree conditions of Bahrain, where wine and liquor flowed and women were far less inhibited than in Saudi Arabia.

In other words, the new enterprise was to be a sophisticated influence operation, an attempt to project Saudi "soft power" and propaganda on the Aljazeera model.

It took a while for Al-Arab to get organized. As fate would have it, just a week before its scheduled commencement of broadcasting in early 2015, King Abdullah, the Saudi monarch who had authorized the project, died. And on the very day Al-Arab went live, Bahraini government authorities arrived unexpectedly to shut it down. This must have been on orders of the new Saudi ruler, King Salman. It seems he was not confident the new enterprise, bankrolled by his jet-setting nephew the "super-investor" Prince Alwaleed bin Talal, would be sufficiently loyal to the new monarch's interests.

In late 2017, by which time the king's son Mohammed bin Salman had become crown prince and de facto ruler of the kingdom, the regime staged a dramatic crackdown allegedly to curb corruption, arresting and detaining Prince Alwaleed and other Saudi billionaires in the Riyadh Ritz-Carlton.

With his patron incarcerated, Jamal Khashoggi left the country. He made his way to Washington, D.C., where he had cultivated relationships with mainstream media bigshots. He arranged to write columns for the *Washington Post*, criticizing the same harsh and anti-democratic conditions in his home country that he had spent his whole previous career artfully covering up. Khashoggi completely changed his tune, but the only thing that had changed in Saudi Arabia was that Khashoggi's faction in the Saudi power structure was no longer on top.

Following his assassination inside the Saudi consulate in Istanbul, Khashoggi was made into an unlikely martyr for press freedom. *Time* magazine called him a "lonely exile" and put his face on its cover, naming him 2018 Person of the Year, together with some lesser-known writers and broadcasters also killed during the year.

"The stout man with the gray goatee and the gentle demeanor dared to disagree with his country's government," *Time* said. "He told the world the truth about its brutality toward those who would speak out. And he was murdered for it."

With prose of deepest purple, *Time* continued: "But the crime would not have remained atop the world news for two months if not for the epic themes that Khashoggi himself was ever alert to, and spent his life placing before the public."

This last statement is demonstrably false. Khashoggi was, at least before November 2017, a lifelong influence agent, intelligence operative, and propagandist for the Saudi regime.

In an age plagued by Fake News, *Time* magazine, without a hint of irony or self-awareness, canonized and placed on its cover a Fake Newsman.

Was Khashoggi, after his faction fell from favor, in any fashion a sincere convert to a radically different system of government from that which had enriched and empowered him all his life? Was he really a "lonely exile" and a quixotic voice for democracy and human rights?

Here is why that is extremely unlikely. It would be out of character for Jamal Khashoggi. He was highly informed, intelligent, and practical. He understood the real situation of Saudi Arabia much better than the American readers whom he was systematically misleading. And the situation is this: No matter how much a person with Khashoggi's prominence might agitate for the introduction of democracy into Saudi governance, there is no chance it will happen. Democracy is something the

Saudi rulers call "crossing a red line." They will consider or implement other liberalizing reforms, but not democracy. They refuse to make themselves susceptible to being voted out of office.

Another problem with pretending that democracy can be introduced soon or effectively in Saudi Arabia is that there is no culture to support democracy. Westerners can deplore that as much as it may make us feel good to do so, but it does not change reality.

Almost certainly Khashoggi's *Washington Post* columns and his other acts of agitation were in service not to idealistic visions of liberalism and democracy but to interests aligned with the Muslim Brotherhood, possibly including the governments of Turkey and Qatar as well as one or another faction of the Saudi power structure. In both Arabia and Washington, Khashoggi the "journalist" had an attractive, avuncular manner, evocative of an Arab Walter Cronkite saying "that's the way it is" – with one key difference: Most of what Khashoggi said was the way it wasn't.

John R. Bradley is a British journalist with long experience in the Arab world, including several years working as a newspaper colleague of Khashoggi's in Saudi Arabia. His columns in the London *Spectator* on the Khashoggi affair deserve attention. Bradley clearly is no apologist for the Saudi royal family, but he emphatically says that Khashoggi was a Saudi intelligence operative and never an independent journalist.

Unlike his naïve *Washington Post* readers, Khashoggi knew that his pronouncements

---

In an age plagued by Fake News,
Time, *without a hint of irony*
or self-awareness, canonized
and placed on its cover
a Fake Newsman.

---

could not bring about liberalization, and certainly not democracy, in Saudi Arabia. He knew very well that the only possible consequence of success in what was to be his final project – stridently criticizing the current Saudi ruler – would have been to weaken the ruler or bring about his downfall and replacement by another Saudi prince.

Prince Mohammed's successor, whether he takes power five minutes or five decades from now, will be another Saudi prince, and the world won't know whether or not it likes his regime until it's experienced it.

Unless, of course, the Saud family dynasty is overthrown.

The overthrow of the Saudi monarchy is something for which no sane person should hope. This does not necessarily mean that the Saudi monarchy is good. It does not mean that the world should love it or unduly praise it. But the world needs to live with it. The only possible alternative to the Saud family dynasty would be so much worse that it likely would bring about a global catastrophe – hundreds of thousands of innocent women, men, and children dead in Arabia and a collapse of the petroleum-dependent world economy. This is not an exaggeration. Iraq and Libya will have been Sunday school picnics compared with the bloodshed and anarchy of an Islamic Republic of Wahhabi Arabia.

Insisting that Khashoggi's murder was an attack on global freedom of the press, journalistic integrity, and prospects for more humane regimes in the Middle East is dangerous self-delusion.

Those who believe the propaganda from the First Amendment-protected American mainstream media may be fooled by their Khashoggi narrative, but, ironically, in the Middle East, people know better. That is because the people of that region know how to read deeply between the lines. People who cope with severely limited political freedom and information are often much wiser and more discerning of reality than the pampered denizens of the Western democracies, drowning in oceans of real information mingled with rivers of disinformation. Middle Easterners should not be condescended to. They should be respected for understanding themselves, their cultures, and their regimes.

Arab Dynasties and Their Rivals

The U.S.-Saudi relationship is not hermetically sealed. It is fully exposed to a volatile external world where both allies and enemies are in close proximity to the Saudi population and oil reserves.

Saudi Arabia remains vital to U.S. security even though the United States has become a net exporter of crude oil. This is because Saudi Arabia, being the only major oil producer with what is known as spare capacity, still has tremendous power to determine world oil prices. The United States follows world prices whether it imports or exports. Make no mistake, it is very good news for the U.S. balance of trade and our energy security for us now to be net exporters, but even that welcome development does not allow us the luxury of isolation from the complex world energy economy.

Because crude oil comes in different grades and because supply and demand vary according to the end products of the different segments of the oil market, the United States still imports large quantities of oil from Saudi Arabia and other countries. Again, what is great news is that we are a *net* oil exporter and are no longer making huge net transfers of wealth to foreign producers.

Meanwhile, other major industrial countries are still heavily dependent upon imports from Saudi Arabia and the other major Middle Eastern oil producers. Japan and South Korea, with virtually no oil reserves of their own, are important in this regard.

Central to the Khashoggi drama is the role of Turkey and its Islamist president, Recep Tayyip Erdoğan. Erdoğan was driving the massive publicity of Khashoggi's disappearance and death even as the events were unfolding.

The Turkish intelligence agency was feeding Western media reports on what was said

Democracy is something the Saudi rulers call "crossing a red line." They refuse to make themselves susceptible to being voted out of office.

to have gone on in the Saudi consulate in Istanbul almost as soon as it happened. This means that the Turks had, or want people to believe they had, real-time eavesdropping inside the Saudi consulate. Had the Turks outwitted the Saudis by installing undetected bugs or was Khashoggi wearing a wire?

The eavesdropping in itself is enough to make one wonder whether the Turks could have intervened to save Khashoggi's life had they wanted to. Since Khashoggi's death being pinned on the Saudi crown prince is one of the best things that has ever happened for Erdoğan's regime, it is understandable why the Turks might have encouraged Khashoggi to enter the Saudi consulate on that fateful day. Round-the-clock Khashoggi coverage including the *Time* magazine cover also helps Erdoğan by overshadowing the international Committee to Protect Journalists' December 2018 annual report naming Turkey the world's worst violator of journalists' rights.

As has been stated already, there is a self-evident case to be made that Jamal Khashoggi was assassinated in a "targeted killing" by the Saudi government because, formerly a reliable Saudi intelligence operative, he had become a renegade.

It is also worth examining whether Khashoggi had been operating in Washington as an unregistered foreign agent of Turkey, Qatar, or both. Circumstances suggest he may have been working in collaboration with Turkish intelligence, while reporting in *The Federalist* suggests he was taking direction from the government of Qatar. Both Turkey and Qatar are aligned with the Muslim Brotherhood against Saudi Arabia. It would be illuminating for public understanding if the Trump administration were to report, for instance, that there is enough evidence that he was an unregistered Turkish or Qatari agent that, had he lived, he could have been prosecuted for violating the Foreign Agents Registration Act.

Saudi-Turkish rivalry has a long history. It predates the NATO alliance, Zionism, the discovery of oil, Atatürk, and even the existence of the United States of America.

Today's Kingdom of Saudi Arabia is the third iteration of Saud family rule over much of the Arabian Peninsula since the dynasty's founding in 1744, when Thomas Jefferson was a British colonial subject and one-year-old infant. The Saud family comes from the center of the peninsula, a sandy, arid, landlocked region called the Nejd whose principal settlement today is Riyadh, a former hamlet now grown into a megalopolis. The Nejd was under nominal rule of the Ottoman Empire for many centuries. Each of the Saudi dynasties aligned its temporal power with a strict, purifying religious movement founded by the scholar Muhammad ibn-Abdul Wahhab – hence today's term Wahhabism, considered pejorative by the Saudis. The Saudis' religious doctrines challenged the orthodoxy and authority of the Ottoman sultans who asserted that they were the true caliphs – successors – of the Prophet Mohammed.

The Saudi heartland was so remote, inhospitable, sparsely populated, and lacking in opportunities for production and commerce to contribute to the empire that the Ottoman bureaucracy largely left it alone. Meanwhile the 18th-century Saud sheikhs had ambitions that could be described, in today's jargon, as liberation from Turkish imperialism, Arab national self-determination, or perhaps even "Make Arabia Great Again."

Only when Saudi chieftains began to attempt, in some instances temporarily succeeding, to conquer the Muslim holy cities of Mecca and Medina to the west of the Nejd in the region called the Hejaz did the Ottomans react. Each of the first two Saudi dynasties was crushed by Ottoman military expeditions. The final ruler of the first Saudi dynasty was captured exactly two centuries ago in 1818, taken to the Sublime Porte, tried and convicted – not of treason but heresy – and beheaded there by the Ottoman overlords.

Middle Eastern people have long memories. Every one of the thousands of princes and princesses of today's Saudi regime remembers this bloody slaying of his or her royal ancestor at the hands of the Turks as vividly as though it happened yesterday.

The third and current Saudi dynastic regime was formed and consolidated during the early part of the 20th century out of the political vacuum left by the collapse of the Ottoman Empire. There is no, and never has been, great love between the Saudi Arabs and the Turks.

Saudi Arabia's closest regional allies are also dynastic regimes. The United Arab Emirates is a federation of seven principalities (emirates) along the Persian Gulf coast, bordering Saudi Arabia and Oman by land, and situated across the gulf from Iran. Each emirate is ruled by a separate hereditary dynasty. The seven dynastic regimes combine to form a single "nation-state" for purposes of foreign and military policy, membership in the United Nations and other international organizations, and some aspects of federal government within the UAE, for example, national highways and other public works.

According to the UAE constitution, the hereditary ruler of Abu Dhabi is *ex officio* the federal president and the ruler of Dubai is prime minister. These two emirates are the wealthiest and most influential of the seven, Abu Dhabi by virtue of oil and gas riches and Dubai because of its status as an international port, financial center, and travel destination comparable to Singapore and Hong Kong.

Saudi Arabia leads an international organization of Gulf Arab states called the Gulf Cooperation Council. The UAE is the second-most-powerful GCC member. Kuwait, Bahrain, Oman, and Qatar are the other members. Tiny Bahrain's foreign policy is not merely aligned with but is essentially determined by Saudi Arabia's. The other GCC states are truly independent of Saudi Arabia's policies, and at the moment, one of them – Qatar – is an antagonist.

With vast reserves of natural gas, Qatar is fabulously wealthy on a per-capita basis. Over the GCC's history, it often has been on good terms with Saudi Arabia, but today the two countries are in conflict. Saudi Prince Mohammed sees Qatar as too closely involved with the radical Islamist Muslim Brotherhood and too friendly with Iran. In 2017, Saudi Arabia, the UAE, and Egypt cut diplomatic, trade, and transportation ties with Qatar. Oman, which practices the Ibadi sect of Islam – neither Shia nor Sunni – often plays a mediating role between Iran and the Sunni Gulf Arab states. Kuwait, so well-known when it was captured by and later liberated from Saddam Hussein, does not play as prominent a diplomatic role as Saudi Arabia and the UAE.

Egypt is neither a Gulf Arab state nor a monarchy, but its succession of military governments – with the interval of a democratically elected Muslim Brotherhood government – resembles a dynasty. Egypt, Saudi Arabia, and the UAE are closely aligned in regional conflicts versus Shia Iran and Iran's clients and co-religionists, the Houthi in Yemen, Hezbollah in Lebanon, and the Assad regime in Syria.

Insisting that Khashoggi's murder was an attack on global freedom of the press, journalistic integrity, and prospects for more humane regimes in the Middle East is dangerous self-delusion.

All the regimes mentioned above, both allies and adversaries of the United States, are autocratic, some more so than others. All these friendly or unfriendly Muslim autocracies commit extrajudicial killings out of *raisons d'état.* And, remember, so do the Israelis, and so do we.

The animosities among several important U.S. allies present huge challenges to our president and his diplomats. A president with responsibility for optimizing relations with allies needs to try to keep both Turkey and Saudi Arabia on the best possible terms with the United States, even when the Saudi-Turkish relationship is at its nadir. Our president must do likewise when wealthy Qatar – home to a U.S. Air Force base – is under embargo by Saudi Arabia, the UAE, Egypt, and little Bahrain, which hosts the headquarters of the U.S. Navy's Fifth Fleet, just a short strait away from Qatar.

The U.S. president also has much at stake now at a sensitive moment for Israeli-Arab diplomacy. Saudi Arabia and the UAE are indicating friendly and cooperative de facto relations with Israel, with a real prospect for future formal relations.

The Constitution makes clear that diplomacy is a power reserved to the executive branch. Puerile gestures by members of the legislative branch make the president's task all the more difficult.

Jeane Kirkpatrick's Lessons Still Apply

Jeane Kirkpatrick was a wise and mature scholar, teacher, and writer on political science and international relations when she wrote her famous essay for *Commentary*, "Dictatorships and Double Standards," in November 1979. She was a lifelong Democrat who had been comfortable for most of her adult life as a "Cold War liberal."

Disaffection first with the McGovernites' capture of the Democratic party leadership in 1972 and later the fecklessness of President Jimmy Carter's foreign policy led Kirkpatrick to become harshly critical of the Democratic left wing in general and leftist and Carterite foreign policy in particular.

Ronald Reagan, running for president

against Carter in 1980, read the Kirkpatrick article on the advice of his foreign policy aide Richard Allen. So impressed was Reagan that he asked Kirkpatrick to become one of his campaign's top foreign affairs advisers. She accepted and following Reagan's election became a transformational figure as his ambassador to the United Nations.

The two crises prompting Kirkpatrick to write her essay were the overthrow of the authoritarian Iranian monarchy of Mohammad Reza Shah Pahlavi by the Shia Muslim revolutionaries of Ayatollah Ruhollah Khomeini and the ouster of Nicaragua's autocratic Somoza regime by the Sandinistas, the first Marxist movement to take power on the American continent.

The Nicaraguan revolution threatened to strengthen the Cuban Castro regime's capabilities while possibly directly installing Soviet troops and missiles on the American mainland during a time of the greatest expanse of the worldwide Soviet empire.

The shah's downfall brought to power a virulently anti-American regime where formerly there had been a close alliance in a powerful, populous, strategically placed country. Saudi Arabia, despite being the center of Sunni Islam, had enjoyed a cordial and normal relationship with the shah's not-very-religious-reign over a Shia population.

Khomeini's revolution was deeply antagonistic towards Saudi Arabia because of religious differences. The revolution unnerved the Saudi leadership and made them turn towards more severe expressions of Sunni Islam; another motive for the Saudi move towards more stringent religious practice was to outflank Sunni extremists including the Muslim Brotherhood and radical elements within Saudi Arabia that later gave rise to Osama bin Laden's Al Qaeda.

Khomeini's theocracy did not support the atheistic Soviet regime, but Khomeini's obsession with the United States as the "Great Satan" and the expulsion of American military and intelligence personnel and facilities from Iran dealt a severe blow to U.S. effectiveness against the Soviets.

With this as the background for Jeane Kirkpatrick's essay of 40 years ago, and even with the Soviet empire having collapsed 30 years ago, her keen observations remain remarkably relevant today. Her insights apply to how Western hard-leftists and even softer liberals and neoconservatives tend to undermine Western security while failing to deliver the human rights progress they claim to want in the non-Western world.

The entire essay, nearly 10,000 words long, is a masterpiece that should be read and re-read. It is online at the *Commentary* magazine website.

"The Shah and Somoza," Kirkpatrick wrote,

> *were not only anti-Communist, they were positively friendly to the U.S., sending their sons and others to be educated in our universities, voting with us in the United Nations, and regularly supporting American interests and positions even when these entailed personal and political cost.*

Liberals were determined to oust these authoritarian American allies no matter the consequences, Kirkpatrick wrote:

> *… the Carter administration brought to the crises in Iran and Nicaragua several common assumptions each of which played a major role in hastening the victory of even more repressive dictatorships than had been in place before. These were, first, the belief that there existed at the moment of crisis a democratic alternative to the incumbent government; second, the belief that the continuation of the status quo was not possible; third, the belief that any change, including the establishment of a government headed by self-styled Marxist revolutionaries, was preferable to the present government. Each of these beliefs was (and is) widely shared in the liberal community generally. Not one of them can withstand close scrutiny.*

What Kirkpatrick said here about the temptation of allowing Marxists to overthrow traditional authoritarians applies just as much today to the possibility of allowing Saudi

Diplomacy is a power reserved to the executive branch.

Arabia and the other Arab Gulf nations to come under the rule of the Muslim Brotherhood.

Ambassador Kirkpatrick discerned an American mindset that is resistant to foreign policy realism, and these words are just as relevant to the attitudes in Washington today as they were four decades ago:

> *Although most governments in the world are, as they always have been, autocracies of one kind or another, no idea holds greater sway in the mind of educated Americans than the belief that it is possible to democratize governments, anytime, anywhere, under any circumstances. This notion is belied by an enormous body of evidence based on the experience of dozens of countries which have attempted with more or less (usually less) success to move from autocratic to democratic government. Many of the wisest political*

scientists of this and previous centuries agree that democratic institutions are especially difficult to establish and maintain – because they make heavy demands on all portions of a population and because they depend on complex social, cultural, and economic conditions.

This logic is quite obviously reinforced by the prejudices and preferences of many [*Carter*] *administration officials. Traditional autocracies are, in general and in their very nature, deeply offensive to modern American sensibilities. The notion that public affairs should be ordered on the basis of kinship, friendship, and other personal relations rather than on the basis of objective "rational" standards violates our conception of justice and efficiency. The preference for stability rather than change is also disturbing to Americans whose whole national experience rests on the principles of change, growth, and progress. The extremes of wealth and poverty characteristic of traditional societies also offend us, the more so since the poor are usually very poor and bound to their squalor by a hereditary allocation of role. Moreover, the relative lack of concern of rich, comfortable rulers for the poverty, ignorance, and disease of "their" people is likely to be interpreted by Americans as moral dereliction pure and simple. The truth is that Americans can hardly bear such societies and such rulers. Confronted with them, our vaunted cultural relativism evaporates and we become as censorious as Cotton Mather confronting sin in New England.*

The foreign policy of the Carter administration fails not for lack of good intentions but for lack of realism about the nature of traditional versus revolutionary autocracies and the relation of each to the American national interest.

Double Standards Plaguing Us Today

Two broad categories of double standards undermine U.S. credibility and security today. One has to do explicitly with foreign policy as it is conducted constitutionally by the executive branch, with congressional oversight that could be useful in principle but in practice often is very unhelpful.

"Inconsistencies are a familiar part of politics in most societies," Kirkpatrick wrote. "Usually, however, governments behave hypocritically when their principles conflict with the national interest."

> *What makes the inconsistencies of the Carter administration noteworthy are, first, the administration's moralism, which renders it especially vulnerable to charges of hypocrisy; and, second, the administration's predilection for policies that violate the strategic and economic interests of the United States. The administration's conception of national interest borders on doublethink: it finds friendly powers to be guilty representatives of the status quo and views the triumph of unfriendly groups as beneficial to America's "true interests."*

During the 115th Congress of 2017–2018, the Senate majority was nominally Republican. On foreign policy matters, it had a functional majority of liberals and neoconservatives; this is the coalition that passed the "voice vote" resolution condemning the Saudi crown prince. This functional majority is susceptible to the same criticism Kirkpatrick leveled against the Carter administration.

Let's restate her words, substituting a few terms to fit the situation of the 115th Congress:

> *What makes the inconsistencies of the U.S. Senate noteworthy are, first, the Senate's moralism, which renders it especially vulnerable to charges of hypocrisy; and, second, the Senate's predilection for policies that violate the strategic and economic interests of the United States. The Senate's conception of national interest borders on doublethink: it finds friendly powers, e.g., Saudi Arabia, to be guilty representatives of the status quo and views the triumph of unfriendly groups, e.g., the Muslim Brotherhood / radical Islamist network, as beneficial to America's "true interests."*

Now, it is true that the Senate majority has not explicitly called for the triumph of the Muslim Brotherhood / radical Islamist network, but the effects of its moralistic attack on our Saudi ally amount to almost the same thing.

In two particularly rich but dense paragraphs, Kirkpatrick described several aspects of the epistemological and intellectual fallacies of the foreign policy thinking of America's ruling class:

> [*The modernization paradigm is inadequate*] *as a framework for thinking about foreign policy, where its principal effects are to encourage the view that events are manifestations of deep historical forces which cannot be controlled and that the best any government can do is to serve as a "midwife" to history, helping events to move where they are already headed.*
>
> *This perspective on contemporary events is optimistic in the sense that it foresees continuing human progress; deterministic in the sense that it perceives events as fixed by processes over which persons and policies can have but little influence; moralistic in the sense that it perceives history and U.S. policy as having moral ends; cosmopolitan in the sense that it attempts to view*

the world not from the perspective of American interests or intentions but from the perspective of the modernizing nation.

The perennial wisdom of Kirkpatrick's "America First" realism, as opposed to today's alliance of leftist and neoconservative moralists, is vital to the reconstruction of a sound American foreign policy based on national interests. If one would pardon the expression, one even might call it a lodestar.

The second broad category of double standards undermining American security has to do with the rule of law as it is so inconsistently applied to cases of unauthorized disclosures of classified national security information.

The instances are myriad. One example is the case of David Petraeus, the much-bemedaled darling of Davos who served no jail time and was allowed to plead to a misdemeanor charge that did not reflect the gravity of his offense, giving classified information to his lover/biographer. Here was an opportunity for our justice system to place a severe penalty on the reckless, faithless, grandiosely self-serving former director of central intelligence. Here was a chance to get it right when dealing with betrayal of secrets at the highest level of government. But Petraeus – who curiously is a neoconservative favorite even though he discernibly believes in nothing except his own ambition – was allowed to walk away.

In late 2018, the Khashoggi media conflagration was spreading faster than a California wildfire when the *Washington Post* published a report purported to be the CIA's secret analysis – opinion based on facts or rumors collected with varying levels of "confidence" – proving, the *Post* claimed, that the Saudi crown prince personally ordered the assassination. More than likely the *Washington Post* received

---

Big Media doesn't always have to name a clandestine agent to blow his cover.

---

the top-secret document before it was conveyed to President Trump.

Trump and his administration were put on the defensive by the media and the usual Senate suspects. Why, the cosmopolis of leftists and neoconservatives demanded, had the president not severed relations with Saudi Arabia or called on its ruler to be deposed?

Meanwhile in flyover country, ordinary citizens should have been wondering: Why hasn't Trump fired the director of the CIA? After all, she's not exactly a MAGA activist. She's a career spook, a Langley lifer. What should be the consequences of her ineffectiveness at controlling leaks?

Yet another example is that of James Wolfe, the Senate Select Committee on Intelligence chief of security who was caught leaking extremely sensitive FISA court information to his paramour, a college student journalism intern, Ali Watkins, 32 years his junior. Thanks to Wolfe's criminal activity, she scored a scoop that made her a finalist for the Pulitzer Prize when she was still a senior in college. After graduation, in one of the most rapid rises ever recorded, she became a *New York Times* national security correspondent.

Prosecutors recommended that Wolfe serve two years in prison. The Republican committee chairman Richard Burr of North Carolina and the Democratic vice chairman Mark Warner of Virginia implored the judge to let Wolfe off with no jail time. Obama-era director of national intelligence James Clapper also petitioned the judge for leniency for Wolfe.

In a rebuke not only to Wolfe but to his Senate and Deep State patrons, U.S. District Judge Ketanji Brown Jackson sentenced him to two months behind bars.

Wolfe was the villain in the apparent violation of Trump campaign adviser Carter Page's civil rights in the sleazy "Steele dossier" matter. Wolfe's crime struck at the very heart of what is supposed to be a system of protecting national security information and protecting American citizens from unwarranted police-state persecution.

Wolfe had been able to avoid trial and possible jeopardy for a heavier sentence by striking a plea bargain. He gained this easier treatment because his lawyers threatened to subpoena every Senate Select Intelligence Committee member to testify had there been a trial.

It's easy to see why Burr and Warner didn't want that to happen.

What did Burr and Warner know about Wolfe, Watkins, and the betrayal of highly classified secrets? When did they know it? What were they afraid to say under oath in open court?

Maybe North Carolinians and Virginians don't care about their senators' behavior, but foreign governments do. Our adversaries are salivating at the smorgasbord of state secrets that will become available to them because our dysfunctional government is not willing to keep them secret. American allies, too, have taken note of the conduct of Petraeus, Burr, and Warner – and they will be less and less inclined to cooperate with the United States if doing so could undermine their own national security.

When the *Washington Post* isn't busy blowing the covers of untold numbers of clandestine agents – with no apparent regard for how many deaths this might cause – the newspaper channels its inner J. Edgar Hoover to protect the cover of spooks whose actions serve the *Post's* political agenda. Such was the case when Tucker Carlson's *Daily Caller* reported in May 2018 that Stefan Halper, an American with a sinecure at Cambridge University, had been an FBI spy allegedly seeking to entrap some Trump campaign advisers as having untoward dealings with Russians.

Before Halper had been identified by the *Daily Caller*, the *Post* had published leaks from Halper and warned readers that "the stakes are so high" for Halper, who was still anonymous at the time, "that the FBI has been working over the past two weeks to mitigate the potential damage if the source's identity is revealed." The *New York Times* also published leaks derived from Halper's spying and declined to name him because it "typically does not name informants to preserve their safety."

If it had not been for the *Times* and the *Post* and their friends in the FBI, how could the world have known that Tucker Carlson and his *Daily Caller* were the Julius and Ethel Rosenberg of the 21st century? Meanwhile Stefan Halper bravely continues to enjoy his sherry and Yorkshire puddings, as yet unscathed in his Cambridge chair.

Let it be noted too that Big Media don't always have to name a clandestine agent to blow his cover. A certain amount of information allows hostile foreign intelligence agencies to connect the dots, often with deadly consequences for the exposed agent.

Another double standard undermining both the rule of law and national security is the amount of protection accorded to broadcasting and publishing companies when illegally disclosed state secrets get into those companies' possession.

The architects of the Bill of Rights surely did not foresee an environment in which huge national and multinational media corporations with armies of highly paid lawyers could traffic in state secrets with impunity because they invoked the First Amendment.

The decentralization of communications, including the advent of social media, makes the folly and injustice of giving big corporations a First Amendment defense for trafficking in classified secrets all the more apparent. In a technological age when everyone with a smartphone is a publisher and broadcaster, why shouldn't everyone have a First Amendment-protected right to commit espionage or treason?

Trump forcefully attacked what Kirkpatrick would have called the optimism, determinism, moralism, and cosmopolitanism of Bush-Graham-Rubio.

There is a lot of work here for those committed to a jurisprudence of "original intent."

While Americans may refuse to pay attention to these problems, be assured that both our adversaries and the endangered species known as American allies are taking notes and learning lessons.

What Is To Be Done?

Rank-and-file Republican primary voters in 2016 resoundingly rejected the essentially identical foreign policy platforms of candidates Jeb Bush, Lindsey Graham, and Marco Rubio. Simply put, these platforms called for renewing the George W. Bush administration's prescription of sentimental humanitarianism and militarism – at a higher dose.

Donald Trump, in more plain-spoken language than Kirkpatrick's, forcefully attacked what she would have called the optimism, determinism, moralism, and cosmopolitanism of Bush-Graham-Rubio.

Trump scored overwhelming victories in

the primaries, including those in Bush and Rubio's Florida and Graham's South Carolina. To the disbelief of his primary opponents, Trump won not only the nomination but the general election.

Putting Trump's mandate for foreign policy change into practice has been difficult because most Republicans who have made a career out of foreign policy since the end of the Reagan administration and the fall of the Soviet empire have been heavily conditioned by the neoconservative project of a "lite" version of liberal optimism, determinism, moralism, and cosmopolitanism.

Trump's first secretary of state was a cosmopolitan corporate bureaucrat. Trump's first ambassador to the U.N. was an extravagantly ambitious moralist who had denounced Trump as unfit for the presidency while she campaigned for Marco Rubio in the 2016 primaries. She used her position at the U.N. primarily to promote herself as a candidate for president in 2024, or perhaps as a primary challenger to Trump in 2020. Trump's second national security adviser, after the three-week tenure of Michael Flynn, was a deterministic Petraeus acolyte, like his mentor a pseudo-intellectual apple polisher.

It's not yet clear whether the new appointees to those posts will actually deliver a realistic foreign policy for the president. If they do, they will need to work hard to staff our embassies and State Department bureaus with realists. This is a tall order, but it must be done.

The Senate of the 116th Congress is off to a disappointing start. With Corker and Flake having departed, there were hopes of more realism from this body. Regrettably, the Senate still has a functional leftist-neoconservative majority. This was made dismayingly evident in the January 31 vote in favor of Majority Leader McConnell's resolution characterized as a "rebuke" to President Trump on national security policy.

McConnell's resolution undermines the commander-in-chief regarding our military role in Afghanistan and Syria. It also takes the side of the permanent intelligence bureaucracy against the president. Trump has expressed skepticism about reports from the national intelligence agencies. They are supposed to work for the president, but McConnell is more comfortable if the president is subservient to them. That arrangement perpetuates the Iron Triangle.

The Iron Triangle is a political science term for the combination of Congress, the permanent federal bureaucracy, and special interest groups to thwart presidential effectiveness; sometimes those special interest groups include the ideologically leftist mainstream media.

The struggle between Trump and the woefully large number of anti-Trump Republicans in the Senate is not really about the true constitutional separation of powers. McConnell and crew are not standing up for the rightful power of the legislative branch as the Framers intended; they are shilling for the Iron Triangle.

There is no clearer sign of hubris than this: Establishment Senate Republicans are panicking and breaking with the president because, as of the date of the vote on McConnell's resolution, Trump's approval-disapproval rating was 42%-55%.

Autocracies won't listen to our lecturing about the rule of law if we don't follow it at home.

And what was the approval-disapproval rating of the GOP Senate geniuses of self-preservation? It was 12%-69%.

The untrustworthy Senate Intelligence Committee is not a disaster waiting to happen; it's a disaster that already has happened. If McConnell were to change course and fight for the president, he could become a national hero. He could help dramatically if he were to lead a process to disband the current intelligence panel and replace it with a newly chartered committee with a completely different membership and staff. It is within his leadership power to orchestrate such a reform.

In any case, President Trump should consider ordering the U.S. intelligence community to cease cooperation with the Senate unless the Senate shows it can be trusted with sensitive information. The status quo is a true crisis of both national security and the constitutional separation of powers.

Autocracies won't listen to our lecturing about the rule of law if we don't follow it at home. America needs to stop national security leaks by punishing not only a few selected bit players but also the big multinational media corporations that callously put our lives and freedom in jeopardy for the sake of profit.

Surely senators leak vital state secrets while hiding behind "separation of powers" to avoid prosecution. How refreshing it would be to put a leaking senator in the dock, *pour encourager les autres.*

Neither autocracies nor democracies will cooperate with us in sensitive intelligence matters if they think that the *Washington Post* and others will publish their secrets, undermining their security and possibly putting the lives of their own operatives in peril.

When we botch democracy, representative government, and the rule of law at home and make a mockery of our own Constitution, why should the ruling family of a functioning Gulf Arab autocratic monarchy consider becoming figureheads and ceding power to an untested constitutional system?

Jeane Kirkpatrick concluded "Dictatorships and Double Standards" with this sentence:

> *Liberal idealism need not be identical with masochism, and need not be incompatible with the defense of freedom and the national interest.*

When she wrote that line, the adversary was the Soviet empire and the model of level-headed liberal idealism was Senator Scoop Jackson, carrying on the intellectual legacy of George Orwell.

Can such a statement be true anymore in a national capital where presidential leadership in foreign policy is hobbled by a bipartisan Senate majority of virtue-signalers?

Anti-Trump Republican senators are gambling that they can ride out a one-term presidency and that things will return in 2021 to the *status quo ante* of George W. Bush foreign policy. They resemble the Republican Old Guard that considered Reagan a fluke and a nuisance and pined for a return to the comfort zone they had enjoyed with Jerry Ford.

This will be an issue for the voters to decide next year. Do they really want a reversion to the George W. Bush era?

Would Republican Senate bosses be wise to run their negative 57% approval rating against Trump's negative 13% approval rating? Would Republican donors be sane to contribute to anti-Trump senators in this environment?

First American edition published in 2019 by Encounter Books, an activity of Encounter for Culture and Education, Inc., a nonprofit, tax exempt corporation.
Encounter Books website address: www.encounterbooks.com

Manufactured in the United States and printed on acid-free paper. The paper used in this publication meets the minimum requirements of ANSI / NISO Z39.48–1992 (R 1997) (*Permanence of Paper*).

FIRST AMERICAN EDITION

LIBRARY OF CONGRESS CATALOGING-IN-PUBLICATION DATA
IS AVAILABLE

10 9 8 7 6 5 4 3 2 1

SERIES DESIGN BY CARL W. SCARBROUGH